The Baroque Guitar

selected and transcribed by
Frederick Noad

Ariel Publications
New York • London • Tokyo • Sydney • Cologne

e d

© Ariel Publications, 1974
A Division of Music Sales Corporation, New York

International Standard Book Number: 0-8256-9951-7
Knopf International Standard Book Number: 0-394-73041-0
Library of Congress Catalog Card Number: 73- 92400

Distributed throughout the world by Music Sales Corporation:

33 West 60th Street, New York 10023
78 Newman Street, London, W1P 3LA
4-26-22 Jingumae, Shibuya-ku, Tokyo 150
27 Clarendon Street, Artarmon, Sydney NSW
Kolner Strasse 199, 5000 Cologne 90

Exclusive book trade distribution for
Alfred A. Knopf, Inc., 201 East 50th Street
New York, New York 10022, in the United States
by Random House, Inc., New York, and
simultaneously in Canada by Random House
of Canada Limited, Toronto.

Book design by Iris Weinstein

Picture research by Jane Dorner
Illustrations on pages 33, 37 and 71
courtesy of Dover Publications, Inc., New York.

Grateful acknowledgement is made to the following
libraries for the use of manuscripts in their possession:
Bayerishce Staatsbibliothek, Munich; The British
Library; Bibliotèque Nationale, Paris; Universität und
Stadtbibliothek, Cologne; Staat und Stadtbibliothek,
Augsburg; Bibliothèque Municipale, Besançon;
Sächsische Landesbibliothek, Dresden; Stift
Kremsmunster, Austria.

Contents

Introduction

The music selected for this collection was composed during the years from 1650 to 1750, representing the middle and late part of the period known as the Baroque. The term, derived probably from the Portugese *barroco,* an irregularly shaped pearl, was originally used in a depreciatory sense to imply an excess of ornament and elaboration in both music and architecture. This is in fact a heritage from the nineteenth century, whose critics and musical audiences had little appreciation for the Baroque style, and whose performers, when they did play the music, often altered the ornaments to avoid the dissonance that is so characteristic of it, and even changed chords and cadences to suit what was then considered good taste. While Dr. Bowdler was carefully eliminating from Shakespeare's works any words considered unsuitable for the young or the fair sex, so music editors were removing the essential spice and jangle from Baroque music.

The result of this Victorian misinformation is that the present compiler must ignore the editorial work of the past century and much of the early part of this one, concentrating on the original manuscripts and publications, attempting to discover from the writings of the composers of the period their real spirit and intention. In the case of this book the search has involved a very extensive survey of the surviving literature for the guitar and lute, with particular attention to such comments as the composers of the period have made on how their music should be played. There is in fact an enormous resource of music surviving from the period, although inevitably much of it is trivial and pedestrian. In addition the composers, who waxed eloquent and expressive to a degree in their dedications to a noble patron, were surprisingly economic of words in their instructions to the player.

1650 found the guitar in a state of increasing popularity following the addition of a fifth pair of strings which considerably increased its range over the four-course Renaissance instrument. It was much easier to play than the lute, to which also at this time extra courses were added to increase the bass range and for which a new tuning became popular under the influence of the French lutenists. The new tuning favored the use of the lute for song accompaniment and the realization of figured basses, but appeared to make it over-complex as an instrument for multi-part counterpoint. The essentially vocally conceived solo lute music of the late Renaissance gave place to simple stylized dances restricted mainly to a treble and bass line with the irregular addition of fuller chords.

In Spain the six-course vihuela had now declined completely, its role in serious music having been superceded by the keyboard instruments. In both Italy and Spain the five-course guitar was popular as a folk instrument, and was employed in two distinctive styles—Rasgueado (strummed) for dance accompaniment, and Punteado (fingered) for the performance of simply conceived solos based mainly on the dance forms.

Although both the guitar and lute were assigned roles of secondary importance in the Baroque period, it is during this same period that the first example of the phenomenon of "guitar mania" occurred, at the court of Charles II. The scene is graphically described in the *Memoirs of the Count of Grammont,* edited by Sir Walter Scott, from which the following is an extract.

> "There was a certain foreigner at court, famous for the guitar, he had a genius for music, and he was the only man who could make anything of the guitar; his style of playing was so full of grace and tenderness that he could have given harmony to the most discordant instruments. The truth is, nothing was too difficult for this foreigner. The King's relish for his compositions had brought the instrument so much into vogue that every person played upon it, well or ill; and you were as like to see a guitar on a lady's dressing table as rouge or patches. The Duke of York played upon it tolerably well, and the Earl of Arran like Francisco* himself. The Francisco had composed a Sarabande which either charmed or infatuated every person; for the whole guitarery at court were trying at it, and God knows what a universal strumming there was."

A similar situation seems to have prevailed in the French court of Louis XIV, the king himself being a player of the instrument. Even Lully, the leading court composer and violinist, was more easily persuaded to perform on the guitar than the violin, a fact that the 18th Century historian Sir John Hawkins regarded with great scorn.

*Francisco Corbetta

The Sources

Both guitar and lute music were written in tablature notation (see below), and for the guitar there is a considerable resource of surviving printed books. Among the most famous and successful of these may be mentioned Gaspar Sanz's *Instruccion de musica sobre la guitarra española*, (Zaragoza 1674), an extensive method with illustrations of the left hand in a number of chord positions, detailed instructions on playing and a number of pieces for performance. The original book was added to and reprinted, and as late as 1752 was extensively copied by Pablo Minguet Y Yrol for his method *Arreglas Y Advertencias*. Admired by Sanz and well-known all over Europe was the Italian guitarist mentioned above, Francesco Corbetta (c1615-1681), who after several previous books published *La Guitare Royale* in 1670 dedicated to Charles II. The book is beautifully engraved and worthy of its royal dedicatee, containing a large selection of solo dance suites and songs, and instructions in French and Italian for the interpretation of tablature. Further books under the same title appeared in 1673 and 1674, evidencing the success of the original.

Corbetta's pupil Robert de Visée became a celebrated musician in his own right, and in 1682 published his first *Livre de Guitare* dedicated to his royal patron Louis XIV. A second collection followed in 1686, and these two books provide a considerable resource for the modern transcriber being clearly engraved in a tablature less elaborate than Corbetta's.

In Italy one of the most interesting publications was Count Lodovico Roncalli's *Capricci armonici sopra la chitarra spagnola*, (Bergamo, 1692) more simply printed than the "royal" books mentioned above, but containing music of great interest. The 1881 transcription of this book by Oscar Chilesotti was one of the first of the modern era, and provided the inspiration for several movements of Respighi's *Suites of Ancient Dances*.

It is beyond the scope of this book to discuss all the guitar publications of the period since they are quite numerous, the British Museum library alone containing more than twenty of them. However it should be mentioned that a fair proportion of them are in the "Rasgueado style" which, since it consists only of simple chord sequences with dance rhythm indications, affords little interest to the player of today.

Printed books for the lute are scarcer than those for the guitar during the Baroque period, giving evidence that the more difficult instrument had less of a popular following. Nevertheless a number have survived, among them Thomas Mace's *Musick's Monument*, published by subscription in London in 1676. This book contains elaborate instructions for playing the lute, together with recommendations for choosing strings, caring for the instrument, design of a music room etc. Much of this old music teacher's personal philosophy emerges from the text, and his impassioned defence of the lute serves to underline the decline in its popularity in England. On the continent the decline was less marked and books continued to appear in France until 1730 and in the German-speaking countries until as late as 1760.

A much greater source of lute music exists in manuscript including all that survives of perhaps the greatest lute composer of his period, Sylvius Leopold Weiss. In spite of contemporary recognition much of Weiss's music still remains to be transcribed into modern notation.

For further information on the books and manuscripts with details of modern editions and transcriptions, the reader is referred to Ernst Pohlmann's *Laute, Theorbe, Chitarrone,* (Edition Eres Lilenthal/Bremen, 2nd Edition, 1972). This is the most complete reference work so far produced on the lute and its music.

The Tablature

The music for both guitar and lute was written in tablature rather than conventional notation. Under this system the lines each represent a string (or rather pair of strings known as a 'course') and either letters or numbers indicate the frets to be fingered by the left hand.

The most usual tuning for the Baroque guitar corresponded to the upper five strings of the modern guitar, i.e.

The example above is given in the form in which guitar music is now written, that is to say transposed up an octave from true pitch. This applies to all musical examples in this book.

The upper three courses were unison strings, the lower two having a higher octave string in each pair, noted above in brackets. Unfortunately this tuning was not universal, the lower two courses containing sometimes unisons on the lower octaves, and at others unisons on the higher, the latter giving a rather curious up and down tuning. The purpose of the high octaves was to add to the fullness of chords, and to enable scale passages to be played with a maximum of open strings, the resultant overringing effect being known as *Campanelas* (Bells).

The tablature does not distinguish between the octaves, and whichever of the above tunings were used the indication for the open courses was

In this form of notation the 'a' stood for the open string, 'b' for the first fret, 'c' for the second fret etc. Thus the passage

would appear in tablature as:

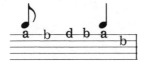

Note that the time was indicated above the lines, and that the time symbols were frequently not repeated for a series of notes of the same value, but only when there was a change to a different time value.

The above example shows the French form of tablature. The Italian tablature employed the same principle, but numbers were used in place of letters, and the highest string of the guitar was represented by the bottom line rather than the top as in French tablature.

The common tuning for the Baroque lute was

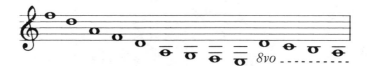

for which the tablature notation was:

The strings below the sixth course were normally played open, and were adjusted chromatically to the key of the individual piece.

The upper strings were commonly in unison pairs, the bass pairs having often a high octave instead of a unison. It should be noted that unlike the guitar the high octave was intended only to add harmonic richness to the low note and was not considered a musical tone in its own right.

For the guitar there was in addition a form of shorthand notation associated principally with the *Rasgueado* style. Common chords were allocated a letter of the alphabet, and simple signs were used to indicate a downward or upward strum. Often this shorthand was used in combination with conventional tablature, a form known as *mixed tablature*.

Space does not permit a discussion of all the intricacies of Baroque tablature because of the many types and the differences in detail even in the same type from one composer to another. But for those interested some facsimiles are included which may be compared with the transcribed versions in this book.

Facsimile of title page and baroque guitar tablature
The gavotte is from *Capricci Armonici Sopra La Chitarra Spagnola* by Lodovico Roncalli, transcribed on page 48. *The Trustees of the British Museum.*

Facsimile of baroque lute tablature
From the manuscript of S. L. Weiss. This piece is transcribed on page 118. *The Trustees of the British Museum.*

Facsimile of Baroque lute tablature.
This shows the First Lute part of the duo by Lauffensteiner transcribed on page 79. *Staatsbibliothek, Augsburg, West Germany.*

Editorial Policy

The versions in this book are offered as performing scores, and differ in some respects from literal transcription intended for academic purposes. This is not to say that wild liberties have been taken with the tablature, but simply that it is recognized that the modern six-string guitar is not the same instrument as either the Baroque guitar or lute, and that changes have been necessary to accommodate the music of the Baroque instruments to the technical capabilities of the present-day guitar. At times this has involved expressing what appears to be the intention of the composer rather that the bare bones of the tablature, and a simple example will serve better than words to illustrate this point. In the works of Corbetta and his pupil de Visée, a cadence will frequently be found such as the following:

The second inversion of the concluding G minor chord is ugly and inconclusive to the ear, and would also have been considered so in the 17th Century. However the G below the staff that would complete the chord was simply not available on the Baroque guitar. Possibly a complete chord on the upper four strings was not considered strong enough; and possibly also the thumb was intended only to strike the upper octave of the pair of strings at the fifth course, omitting the lower D and simply doubling the higher one. But there is no way to know this from the tablature, and on many occasions the selection of only one of the pair of strings would still produce an imperfect chord. What we do know is that de Visée was embarrassed by such apparent solecisms in his guitar scores, and wrote that "the instrument itself is the reason." We also know that when he wrote for the lute with its many extra bass strings he never included this kind of unsatisfactory cadence.

The solution is clearly to add the low G impossible on the Baroque guitar, or according to the demands of the piece to eliminate the low D, either solution being in my opinion correct to the intention of the composer if in a sense a change from what he wrote.

In giving the above example it is not my intention to mystify the reader with the complexities of tablature, but simply to explain how it can be that the same piece of music can appear with slight differences when transcribed by different editors.

Simple accompaniments for the songs have been derived from the figured basses of the original publications. These consisted of the bass line only, with numbers to indicate the required components of the chords although not their exact disposition. In some cases a simple bass line only was available.

Practical Suggestions in Using this Book

The pieces in this book are graded from easier to more difficult, with the exception of the complete suite by S. L. Weiss which is printed in its correct order, but contains movements which are very easy as well as some of considerable challenge. The notes with each piece are important to the amateur and should at least be considered as they may help with a passage of technical difficulty. In particular the suggestions on trills and ornamentation are given to help those unfamiliar with this period, and since this is perhaps a subject which tends to alarm the amateur I feel that a few preliminary notes may serve to explain the comparative simplicity of the basic rules.

MVSICK.
Although the Cannon, and the Churlish Drum—
Haue strooke the Quire mute, and the Organs Dumb:
Yet Musicks Art with Ayre and String, and Voyce
Makes glad the Sad, and Sorrow to Reioyce.

Musick
The lady plays a typical 10 course baroque lute. *The Trustees of the British Museum.*

Trills and Ornaments

Prior to the classical period both vocalists and instrumentalists had a certain freedom to elaborate the written score with a degree of improvisation. The freedom was not absolute, but governed by certain conventions and by the mood and tempo of the piece. In the late Renaissance lute music the principle form of ornamentation was the *division*—the dividing of long notes into shorter ones. In the majority of cases the lute music has these divisions written out in the repeat to a straightforward strain, e.g., *Queen Elizabeth's Galliard* (John Dowland).

1st strain

1st strain repeat

The accent marks show the notes of the first theme, and it will be noticed that the extra notes do not move far in interval from the original melody note and usually progress step-wise to the next one. Where the repeat was not written out in this form the player would be expected to be able to improvise his own divisions, but they would follow the same general style.

In the Baroque Era it became less common to write out such embellishments, and a series of signs were used as a form of shorthand. Also the character of the ornamentation changed influenced by the development of the slur (ligado), and the acceptance and enjoyment of a dischord on an accented beat (for instance the first of the measure), provided that it was quickly resolved into an harmonic sound. As the simplest and in many ways the most fundamental ornament of the period it is important first to understand the *appoggiatura*.

The Appoggiatura

Literally an ornamental note which "leans" on the main note, the appoggiatura added a moment of dissonance by replacing the main note with one normally a step above or below. The dissonance was then resolved by playing the main (harmonic) note. e.g.

Simple melody

Melody ornamented with appoggiatura

Note that the ornament notes were customarily slurred to the main note. The exact length of the "leaning" note varied considerably according to the period, nationality, and context of the music, and for this reason the appoggiaturas have been interpreted and written out to assist the reader and to avoid complexity. In certain cases, where the ornamentation seems perhaps excessive, the signs have been left unrealized so that the player may include or omit them according to his taste. For the appoggiatura the initial note is shown as a small note linked by a slur to the main note, e.g.

The most common realization would be for the initial note to "borrow" half the time of the main note, i.e.

In the case of a dotted main note, the initial note usually borrowed two thirds of its value, i.e.

Written　　　　　　**Played**

However it must be stated that this is by no means a universal rule; for a general outline readers are recommended to study the articles in the Harvard Dictionary of Music by Willi Apel (Harvard University Press).

The most common indications in tablature were

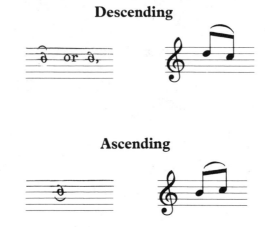

The comma sign in the first example was also used to indicate a trill. It may seem strange that no distinction was made between appoggiatura and trill, but an understanding of the nature of the trill will help to make this clear.

The Trill

Trills may be divided into two main categories; passing trills, which occur in mid-phrase as decoration of a passage, and cadential trills which ornament a final cadence.

Passing Trills

This form of trill is related to the appoggiatura, and simply consists of a dissonant note a second above the main note which is slurred to it. The difference from the appoggiatura is that according to the time available the two notes are repeated a number of times to form a trill.

Interpretation

The reason for the alternative is that the number of notes was not fixed, but depended upon the tempo and character of the phrase, and of course upon the skill of the player. In a fast passage the trill may be simplified to an appoggiatura from the second above.

Interpretation

Note that apart from the first note these trills are all executed with the left hand alone.

Cadential Trills

The cadential trill occurred on the final strong beat preceding the completing chord of a phrase, and consists of the alternation of a dissonant note with its resolution. i.e.

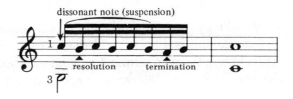

In many ways the cadential trill may be considered as a passing trill with an added termination. As with the passing trill, the number of notes was not fixed and the rhythmic pattern also changed in a number of common formulae.

Abbreviated notation is used in this book, and the above example would appear as:—

However frequent suggestions are given in the study notes for the realization of the trills, and through these the player will become accustomed to the common forms. For variety a number of frequently used formulae are given below.

Written

Played

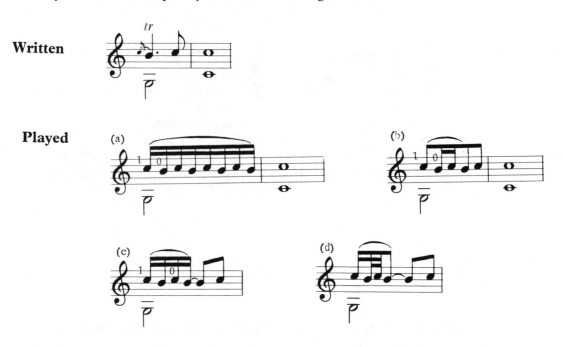

Formula (a) is somewhat ordinary, but appropriate in certain situations. (b) gives more stress to the initial dissonance and is a useful trill that is easy to execute. (c) has the effect of separating the trill more from its termination, and (d) does the same thing with more emphasis on the first note. The following suggestions are particularly recommended to the reader.

1. Try each of the examples above, first slowly to establish the correct time, then more quickly to obtain a neat execution.

2. Note that all trills begin *on the beat* in spite of the way that they are conventionally written.

3. Begin all trills on the *upper* note. The trill beginning on the main note is a later classical form.

4. Remember that the trills are essentially a ligado (slur) technique on the guitar, but that the terminations are not necessarily so and are normally separated from the trill. Even example (a) above could correctly be played with the final C and B detached from the slur.

5. Note that trills between two strings are very rare on the guitar, and are employed only for a special effect or where the alternative would involve excessively awkward fingering.

After the basic principles have been understood experiments may be made to include more notes in the trills or to vary the rhythm. e.g.

The Acciaccatura

Although usually associated with harpsichord music this ornament occurs frequently in music for the baroque lute. Literally a "crushing" sound, it consists of the simultaneous striking of a main note and a note a second below it, the lower note being immediately released. The opening of the Courante by S. L. Weiss illustrates this ornament:

The F♯ and G at the beginning of the measure form the "crushing" dissonance. The immediate release of the lower note is not expressed in the tablature, and is presumed from the similar practice on keyboard instruments.

General

The pieces offered in this book should give an idea of the many different styles existing under the general heading of Baroque. The music for lute and guitar falls into two major divisions; *Arioso* or lyrical style with a singing melody, and *Broken* style consisting of extensive use of the arpeggio. The plucked instruments were particularly suitable for the latter, and indeed contributed materially to the development of this musical technique whereby harmonies and melodies are implied in a succession of single notes.

The collection includes some well-known pieces, which have been carefully checked against original sources and newly fingered for this book. In addition there are many works that have not previously been published in modern guitar editions, which I hope will add materially to the available repertoire.

I have tried to restrict the selections to music of moderate technical difficulty, but the prevailing policy has been to choose works of particular musical attractiveness and interest. This policy has involved travel to many countries, and the reading of literally hundreds of pieces in various forms of notation. The final selection is of course purely a personal one, but it is my sincere hope that the reader will share at least some of the pleasure that I have found in the discovery of this music.

Minuet In G

The library of the Benedictine monastery in Kremsmünster, Austria, contains a valuable collection of manuscript lute books of the 17th and 18th centuries. Many of the works are anonymous, and this minuet from manuscript L. 77 is a typical and melodious example of the vast resource of simple pieces for the baroque lute. From the general contents of the book it may be dated as late 17th or early 18th century.

The minuet of this period may be characterized as an elegant dance form of lively tempo, graceful rather than rapid.

1. *To maintain the simplicity of this piece a trill at this point has been omitted. Players who wish to restore it should finger the passage thus:—*

The same situation applies each time this measure is repeated.
The suggested tempo is ♩ = 120.

Anonymous

Sarabande

This piece is taken from the same source as the preceding and is probably by the same composer since it occurs on the following page and in the same key.

By the late 17th century the sarabande had become a stately and dignified component of the baroque suite, in triple time with frequent stress or prolongation of the second beat of the measure. It is curious that it seems to bear no relationship to the quick dance of the same name which in the late 16th century was banned by Phillip II of Spain because of its lasciviousness.

1 *The stretch between the F♯ and G is awkward but by no means impossible with practice. The resultant clash was common in lute music of the period, adding a welcome touch of spice to the blandness of conventional harmony.*

The suggested tempo is ♩ = 92.

Anonymous

Minuet In E

Adam Falckenhagen was born in 1697 near Leipzig. He was a distinguished player and composed chamber works for lute and strings, in addition to many suites for the solo lute. The latter part of his life was spent in Bayreuth where he held an official appointment as lutenist and chamber musician until his death in 1761.

His works are mostly of simple structure in two voices exhibiting a strong melodic gift. This minuet is taken from a manuscript lute book (Bayerische Stadtsbibliotek. Mus. MS. 5362.), where it appears as *Minuet and Variation*. However it is hard to believe that the variation is other than a simple second part, and I have accordingly printed it below the minuet as an optional accompaniment.

1 *In the manuscript the upper B is doubled, and players may wish to add the extra unison at the fourth fret of the 3rd string, i.e.*

The suggested tempo is ♩ = 108.

Adam Falckenhagen
(1697–1761)

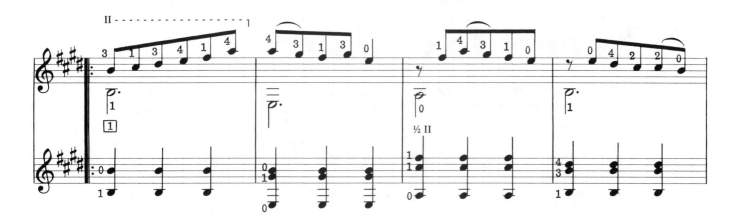

La Lecon de Musique Boucher
The lady sings to the accompaniment of her guitar instructor. At the back of his guitar can be seen the gut frets which were tied around the neck. *W. F. Mansell, Hutchinson & Co. Ltd. (Publishers), 4-7 Red Lion Court, Fleet St. E.C.4.*

Minuet In E Minor

Robert de Visée was both a guitarist and lutenist; a contemporary writer mentions him with both these titles in 1680. The preface to his first book of the guitar (1682) informs us that he had on many occasions played for Louis XIV and the Dauphin, and subsequent court records show him in the King's entourage and much in demand as a player in court concerts, intimate gatherings in Madame de Maintenon's apartments, and the splendid gatherings occasioned by a marriage of the nobility.

After Louis XIV's death he is still listed among the King's chamber musicians, with a wage of 600 livres, and as late as 1716 he published a collection of pieces for the lute or small ensemble.

The salary of 600 livres was not a very grand sum judging from this extract from the contemporary *Journal de Dangeau.*

"Thur 23 October 1704. The King summoned the Prince de Conty to tell him that he was giving a pension of 40,000 livres for his son Count de la Marche. He said he was sorry that it was so little, but that one must start somewhere. On returning from his walk he was present at a concert at Madame de Maintenon's given by Descoteaux, Fourcroy, De Visée and Buterne."

His position was evidently far removed from that of his friend and fellow-musician Lully, who as superintendant of the King's chamber musicians was able to amass a comparative fortune, reputedly leaving 630,000 livres on his death.

This minuet is from de Visée's second book of guitar pieces dated 1686. The suggested tempo is ♩ = 108.

[1] *In the original the two notes of this chord have a diagonal line between them, indicating that the notes would be separated rather than played simultaneously. De Visée is not specific about the amount of separation, which may be taken as a simple slight arpeggiation or, following the custom of the lute players, as halving the value of the notes, e.g.*

The same applies when the chord is repeated in bar 6.

[3] *This cadence represents an approximation of that of the baroque guitar in the example below. The low F♯, representing the lower octave of a double string, would probably not have been sounded for harmonic reasons.*

Minuet In E Minor

Robert de Visée
(c1650–c1725)

The Guitar Player Vermeer
The beautifully detailed painting shows a typical baroque guitar. The position of the hand would indicate that she may be using a plectrum. *The Iveagh Bequest, Kenwood House, Hampstead, London.*

Vivace

There is a pleasant freshness to this piece if it is played at a lively tempo ($\quarternote = 126$). It is in the French *broken style*, depending for interest on typical lute arpeggiation and scales in contrast to the melodic Italian style (for example, the Aria on page 39).

It is technically straightforward except for the two passages noted below.

1. *The change to the third position is necessary for the execution of the scale. This, and the location of the fourth finger on the second string in the following measure, need care and practice.*

2. *It is important to note the fingering of this scale on the fourth and fifth strings. The F♯ and E on the fifth string involve a further change of position, but this prepares the hand for an easy movement to the C♯ which follows. The forte and piano marks should be observed so as to give the echo effect so typical of the period. I have omitted a repeat in the original of the final four measures which does not seem to me necessary or effective.*

Adam Falckenhagen

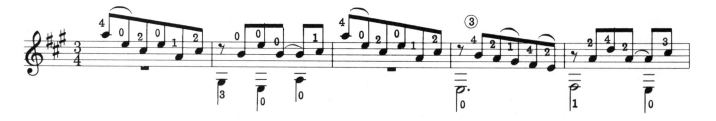

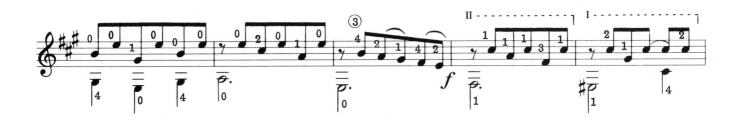

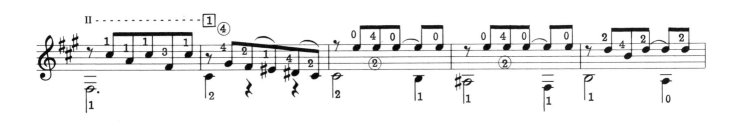

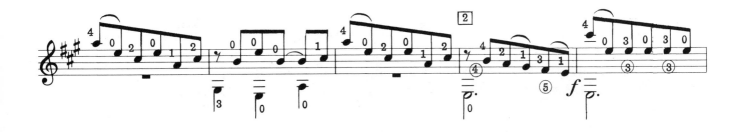

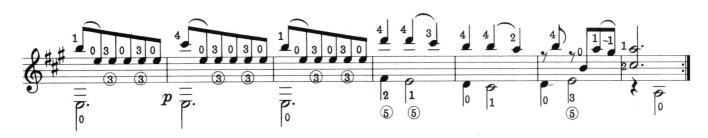

Cancion O Tocata

Santiago de Murcia was a court musician to Phillip V of Spain, and guitar instructor to his first wife, Maria Luisa of Savoy. This piece is taken from a manuscript collection of his pieces dated 1732, and is one of the last examples of guitar tablature before the final decline of interest in the five-course guitar.

I would suggest a lively tempo ($\quarternote$ = 96) and a light hearted approach. The rather nebulous title translates as *Song or Instrumental Piece*.

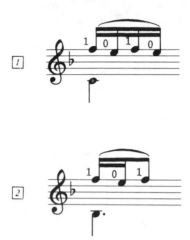

3 *It is important to damp the open A at the end of the measure to prevent an unpleasant over-ring. The right hand thumb is the most convenient to use for this.*

4 *This rather curious fingering facilitates the change to the next chord. The third finger should not leave the string in travelling from the B♭ to the A.*

Santiago de Murcia
(18th Century)

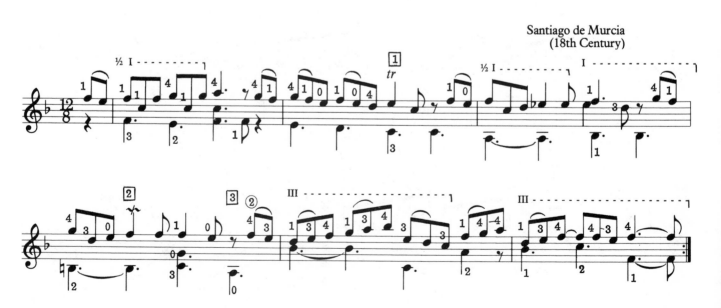

Jean Antoine Mezzetin Watteau
The guitarist's hand indicates that he is playing in the "rasguedo" or strumming style. *The Metropolitan Museum of Art, Munsey Fund, 1934, New York, N. Y. 10028.*

Delicate Beauty

Henry Lawes was one of the leading songwriters during the reign of Charles I; and the most famous poets, amongst them Milton and Waller, competed for the honour of having their verses set to music by him.

Writing in the following century the famous music historian Charles Burney found most of his work "languid and insipid, and equally devoid of learning and genius."

However since Burney also wrote of the great John Dowland that "besides want of melody and design…there are frequent unwarrantable and, to my ear, very offensive combinations in the harmony," one may draw one's own conclusions as to the value of his criticism. In fact Burney's distaste was clearly due to a strong preference for the Italian style of song, whereas Lawes was a particularly English composer.

This charming song is from Lawes' second book of *Ayres and Dialogues* (Playford, 1653). I would suggest a light and fairly fast treatment.

Henry Lawes
(1596–1662)

Suffer in silence I can with delight.
Courting your anger to live in your sight.
Inwardly languish and like my disease,
Always provided my sufferance please.

Take all my comforts in present away.
Let all but the hope of favor decay.
Rich in reversion I'll live as content.
As he to whom fortune her forlock hath lent.

Sarabande In E Minor

In 1692 Count Lodovico Roncalli's *Capricci armonici sopra la guitarra Spagnola* was published in Bergamo, containing nine suites for the five course guitar. The first modern transcription was that of Oscar Chilesotti (Milan 1881), some of whose versions were orchestrated by Respighi for his suites of *Ancient dances and airs.*

While there is much merit in Chilesotti's transcription his failure to realize the correct octaves for the fourth and fifth strings and his frequent omission of appoggiaturas and trills make his work impractical for use as a performing score. However his recognition of the melodic quality and charm of this composer came at a time when this area of music was considered incomprehensible or insignificant.

The short pieces presented in this book are all newly transcribed from the 1692 publication.

The arpeggiated chords are typical of Roncalli's style; and in the period both downward and upward arpeggiation was used. The downward stroke, from bass to treble, was done with the thumb; and the reverse motion from treble to bass with a finger, probably the index. The two initial chords were both thumb strokes, but in the second measure and other passages where the half-note chord is followed by a quarter-note repetition the first was with the finger, i.e.

Playing the chords this way has the effect, clearly intended, of emphasizing the heavy beat and reducing the weak beat almost to an echo.

The first arrows show the full indications of the original and illustrate the style. However it is possibly best left to the player to decide how frequently to use this technique which, although correct for the five course guitar, can seem excessive if used in every case on the modern instrument

For the other trills in the piece I would suggest a similar treatment.

2 *The dissonance and its resolution in this cadence are very typical of both guitar and lute music of this period.*

The suggested tempo is ♩ = 63.

Sarabande In E Minor

Lodovico Roncalli
(17th Century)

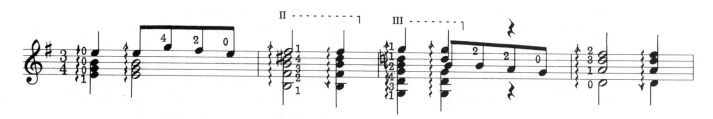

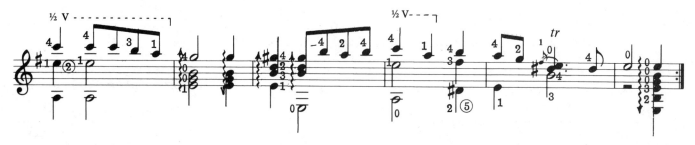

Minuet In A Minor

Purcell wrote a quantity of keyboard music of a simple nature characterized by a song-like melody with an uncomplicated bass, bearing such unpretentious titles as *Song tune, Air, A New Irish tune,* etc. Although not originally intended for it, the structure of these pieces is very similar to many written for the baroque lute, which is perhaps sufficient excuse to include a solo of this distinguished composer.

It is taken from a collection printed for Henry Playford in 1689 entitled *The Second Part of Musick's Hand-maid* where it was printed without title. However it also appears as an anonymous piece under the title of *Minuet* in the 1670 edition of *Apollo's Banquet.*

I would suggest a lively tempo, about ♩ = 104.

Henry Purcell
(c1658–1695)

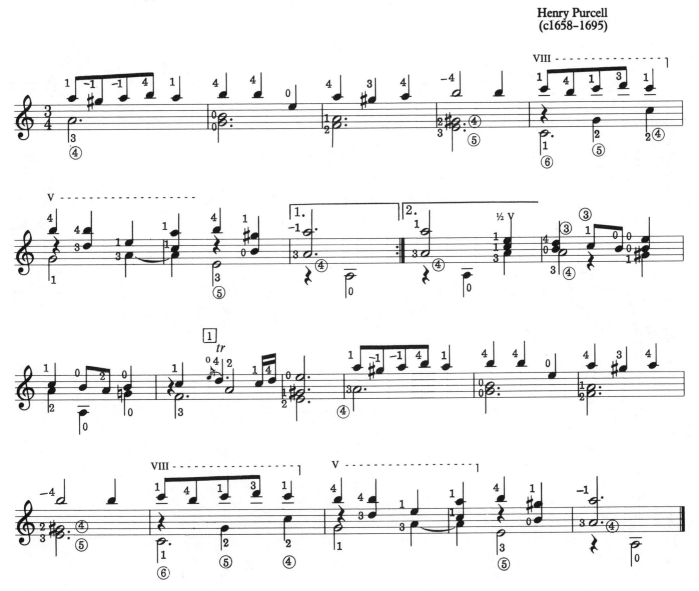

I Prithee Send Me Back My Heart

This song is taken from Henry Lawes' *Ayres and Dialogues, Book III,* published by John Playford in 1658. Information about Lawes is given in the note on p. 28.
I would suggest a light, humourous approach with a moderately fast tempo.

Words by Dr. Henry Hughes

Henry Lawes

lie, to send it me were vain; for th'hast a

thief in ei - ther eye, will steal it back a - gain.

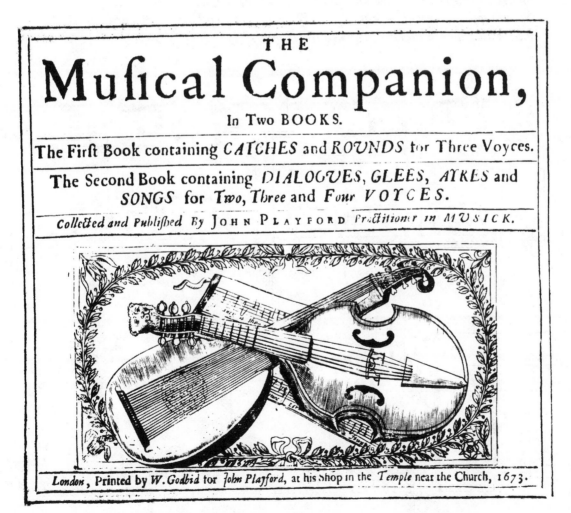

Baroque music printing. Title page of *The Musical Companion* by John Playford, 1673

Gavotte Rondeau

De Visée rarely wrote for two guitars, and this duet is in fact a solo with an optional second part *(contrepartie)*. In spite of this the combination makes a pleasing and spirited encore-type piece. It is taken from a beautifully hand written collection of guitar music of the period now in Paris. (Bibliotheque Nationale Vm7 6222.)

The performance will be effective if both players are careful to do the same type of trill when these ornaments coincide, if necessary giving them special practice to achieve a balance. As the tempo should be somewhat brisk ♩ = 120, I would suggest simple trills, e.g.

2 *Second guitar: The fingering of this scale may seem strange, but if the first finger is held on the C♯ the change to the following chord is very simple.*

3 *Second guitar: These four notes (B to E) were all a step lower in the original. Experiment will show why I have suggested this change.*

Robert de Visée

Minuet In E

This minuet from the lute book mentioned in the note on p. 18, was chosen for its pleasing balance of the melodic and broken styles of composition. The lyrical opening suggests a moderate tempo, about ♩ = 96.

1. *This sequence of chords should be practiced separately to achieve clarity in each of the three voices.*
2. *This measure and the two which follow are slightly more difficult on the guitar than on the lute. The changes of position should be practiced until they are smooth and unhurried.*
3. *Note the typical* repeat in echo *of these two measures.*

Anonymous
(18th Century)

Bourrée

Among the instruments in Bach's collection listed after his death were two lutes and a mechanical instrument known as a *Lautenwerk*. The latter was a form of harpsichord designed by Bach and made for him by the organ builder Zacharias Hildebrand which imitated very exactly the sound of the lute. It is reasonable to suppose that Bach had a working knowledge of the lute, but in view of the difficulty of playing the instrument well on a part-time basis he may have preferred the ease of the keyboard imitation. It is certain that he enjoyed the lute, and when Wilhelm Friedman Bach brought the lutenists S. L. Weiss and J. Kropfgans to see him in July of 1739 it was reported that "something special in the way of music" occurred.

The bourrée below, a most popular piece for guitarists, is from the Suite in E Minor (BWV 996). It occurs in a collection made by Bach's pupil Johann Ludwig Krebs in two staff notation, and a later hand added the words "auf's Lautenwerk."

Suggested tempo is a lively ♩ = 120, and care should be taken to sustain this tempo through the last four or five measures which are slightly more complex than the rest of the piece.

Although by Bach's time the bourrée had become a stylized movement of the baroque suite, it seems to retain the flavour of its origin as a robust French provincial peasant dance.

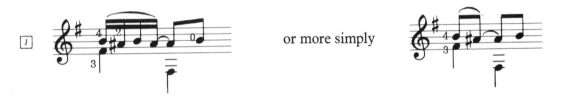

1   or more simply

2 *Note the change of position here, with the B on the sixth string.*

Baroque music printing. Title page of *Frische Clavier Früchte* by Johann Kuhnau

Bourrée

Johann Sebastian Bach
(1685–1750)

Aria

This piece from the Munich lute-book is a free transcription of the aria *Digli che io son fedele* from the Opera *Alessandro nell'Indie* by J. A. Hasse.

Hasse was a native of Germany who went to Naples as a young man and studied under Alessandro Scarlatti. After achieving success and an international reputation in Italy he returned to Germany where he continued composing operas in the Italian style in the employment of the Elector of Saxony. He was married to Faustina, an opera singer of considerable talent and fiery temperament.

Technically straightforward, the aria should provide pleasant and melodious sight-reading practice.

1. *When the fourth finger slides from B to A the hand should move with it in anticipation of the second position bar.*
2. *The ligado from G♯ to F♯ is not as hard as it seems if the 3rd finger is firmly placed in advance. The reason for the fingering is to release the 2nd finger for the B on the 6th string.*
3. *The move to the high C should be precise and unhurried.*

Suggested tempo is ♩ = 76.

Johann Adolf Hasse
(1699–1783)

41

Minuet In Canon

Von Radolt came from a distinguished Vienna family, his father being a high steward in the Emperor's household. His first and only known printed work was entitled *Die Aller Treueste Freindin,* published in Vienna in 1701. It comprised five volumes containing parts for concerted works for three lutes and strings as well as other smaller compositions.

His music shows considerable charm as evidenced by this delightful canon.

1̸ *The original gives a unison here. The suspension is added editorially as it was commonly used in such a situation and would probably be played whether written in or not.*

If careful attention is payed to the fingering the piece should present no technical difficulty.

Suggested tempo is ♩ = 106.

Wenzel von Radolt
(1667–1716)

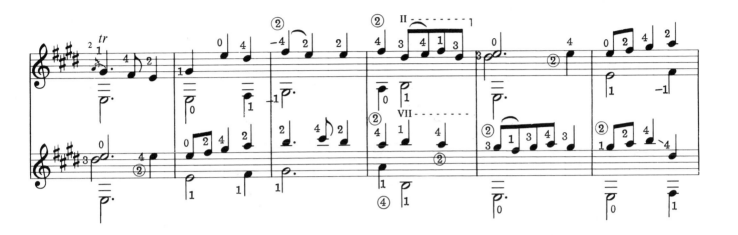

Canon

This further example of von Radolt's work is taken from the same source as the preceding piece. I would suggest playing it at a fast tempo, which seems to make it sound much more interesting and coherent than it does at a leisurely pace.

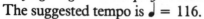 *The trill employing two strings is used in both parts to avoid excessively awkward fingering. The two players should practice for exact synchronization.*

The suggested tempo is ♩ = 116.

Wenzel von Radolt

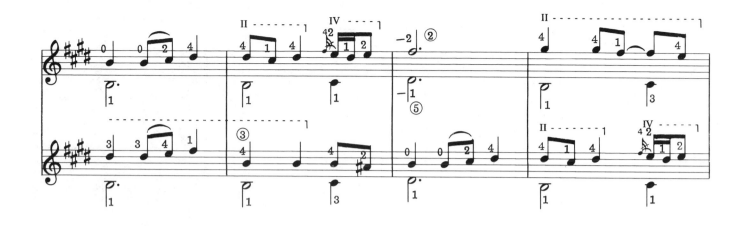

From the title page of *Guitarra Española y Vandola* by Joan Carlos Amat, the first known (1586) method for the five course guitar.

Sarabande In G

This piece and the two which follow are taken from the 1692 publication mentioned in the note on p. 29, which also discusses Roncalli's style of arpeggiation.

1 *Three possibilities are suggested for the trills in this piece, any of which may correctly be used. (a) is the simplest, and quite satisfactory. (b) is a faster version of the same trill, while (c) gives a possible variant by adding prominence to the first note.*

Written

Played

The suggested tempo is a stately ♩ = 76.

Lodovico Roncalli

Gavotte

This gavotte is from the same suite as the preceding Sarabande, and may be paired with it for contrast. It is very lively and even humorous, and for the period a remarkable tune. I would suggest a lively tempo ♩ = 120 with perhaps a tendency to shorten the sixteenth notes which follow the dotted eighths.

1. *This passage in the eighth position forms a short separate statement. I have fingered it with the full bar. If it is played* dolce *(right hand over the sound hole) a contrast may be made with the answering section following, which should be played* metallico *(right hand closer to the bridge).*

2. *It is most important to place the full bar at this point (for the A) in preparation for the following chord.*

3. *In view of the tempo I would suggest a simple trill here, i.e.*

Lodovico Roncalli

48

Gigue

This gigue has great charm and rhythmic variety, and is deservedly one of Roncalli's most popular pieces. I would suggest a bright tempo ♪ = 176.

In the original book it precedes the sarabande on page 47, and the gavotte on page 48.

[1] *I have omitted the trill here which seems to detract from the cadence.*

[3] *Players may prefer* *to the rather hollow effect of the original cadence.*

Lodovico Roncalli

Trio

This trio is from an interesting eighteenth century lute-book now in the Cologne Stadt-bibliothek, which includes compositions by Lauffensteiner, Weiss and others.

The minuet to which it belongs is unfortunately not amenable to transposition, but this seems insufficient reason not to include a delightful duet which stands well by itself.

The key of C minor should not deter the less advanced player as the piece is technically straightforward.

Suggested tempo is ♩ = 104.

Anonymous
(18th Century)

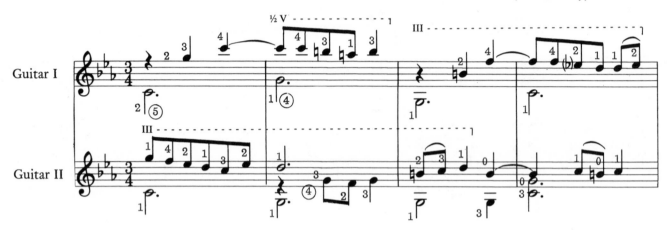

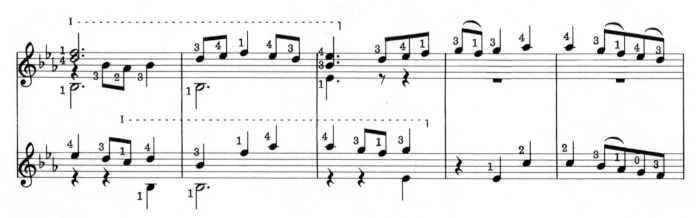

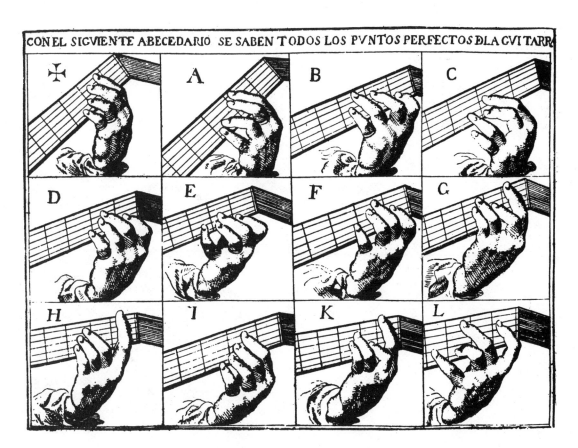

Hand position chart from *Instruccion de Musica Sobre la Guitarra Española* by Gaspar Sanz, 1674

Facsimile of tablature from *Instruccion de Musica Sobre la Guitarra Española* by Gaspar Sanz, 1674

Canarios

One of the interesting treatises on the guitar of the seventeenth century is that of Gaspar Sanz, who describes himself as from the province of Aragon and a bachelor of theology of the University of Salamanca. The book was published in 1674 in Zaragoza with the title *Instrucciòn de Musica Sobre la Guitarra Española,* and contains detailed instructions in technique as well as many musical examples of the dance forms popular in Spain such as *Folias, Españoletas, Rujeros* and the *Canarios* transcribed below.

As with most music written for the baroque guitar it is impossible to re-create the original in a transcription, but the particularly Spanish charm of the dance comes through nevertheless.

1 *The occasional ¾ interspersed with the ⁶⁄₈ is particularly Spanish and rhythmically interesting and effective.*

2 *Note the change from fourth to third finger on the A, necessary for what follows.*
The double bars at the end of each section may be taken as optional, rather than essential, repeats.

Suggested tempo for the dance is ♩.= 112.

Gaspar Sanz
(1640–1710)

Passacaille

In de Visée's book of guitar pieces (1686) this passacaille follows the minuet transcribed on page 22, and may be paired with it for contrast in performance.

It is a very strong piece which lends itself to colorful interpretation. The original statement and its repetitions should be positive so as to throw into relief the more delicate couplets which intervene. Technically quite simple, this is a most rewarding piece to play.

1. *In the original there is a trill between the E and the D♯. For those who wish to play it, the closest approximation to de Visée's intention would probably be:—*

The same situation applies each time this measure is repeated.

2. *There is a repeat at the end of each couplet, marked here by the double bar. I feel that this should be left optional to the player.*

3. *The tablature gives the E and D in the lower voice as eighth notes, the following G as a quarter note. This appears to be a simple printer's error from the logic of the passage.*

4. *For the final cadence players may wish to play the full E minor chord, i.e.*

The French passacaille was a type of rondeau, consisting of a repeated refrain interspersed with varied sections known as "couplets." It should be distinguished from the Passacaglia described in the note on p. 90, and the Passacaille on page 118 of Leopold Weiss which in spite of its French title follows the same general form as the piece on p. 90.
The suggested tempo is ♩ = 80.

Robert de Visée

I Attempt From Love's Sickness To Fly

Henry Purcell was recognized while still a young man as the foremost English musician of his time, and many later historians consider him England's last great composer before the twentieth century. He was a gentleman of the Chapel Royal, and in 1680 succeeded his former teacher Dr. John Blow as organist of Westminster.

This song is from *The Indian Queen*, one of the most important of Purcell's more than fifty operatic works.

The version I have used for this arrangement was published c1695 with the title *A Song in the Indian Queen: as it is now compos'd into an OPERA. By Mr. Henry Purcell. Sung by Mrs. Cross.* About Mrs. Cross, Dr. Burney (see above p. 28) wrote "Mrs. Lindsey, Mrs. Cross, Mr. Good and Mr. Cook had subaltern parts allotted them in early English operas, by which they seem to have contributed but little to their own fame or the pleasure of the public."

It should perhaps be noted that although the guitar accompaniment appears quite simple it calls for sufficient practice to achieve the easy flow required by the melody. The song is usually taken at quite a fast tempo.

Facsimile of Purcell's manuscript. *From his Fantasia Upon One Note,* composed in 1680.

I Attempt From Love's Sickness To Fly

Henry Purcell

I at - tempt from love's _ sick - ness to fly _ in _

vain, since I am my - self my own fe - ver, since I am my -

self my own fe - ver _ and _ pain. No more now, no more now, fond _

heart, with pride no more swell; Thou can'st not _ raise _ forc - es, thou

can'st not_ raise_ forc - es e - nough to re - bel. I at - tempt from love's_

sick - ness to fly _____ in _ vain, since I am my -

self my own fe - ver, since I am my - self my own fe - ver_ and_

pain. For love has more_ pow'r and less mer - cy than fate, to

make us — seek — ru - in, to — make us — seek — ru - in and — love those — that — hate. I at - tempt from love's — sick - ness to fly — in — vain, since I am my - self my own fe - ver, since I am my - self my own fe - ver — and — pain.

Allegro

Although Scarlatti did not write for the guitar his music is a favorite source for guitarists, partly because he was one of the outstanding musical geniuses of his day, and also because the long period he spent in Spain (from 1729 until his death) gave a flavour of Spanish dance music to much of his later work. In addition the essentially two line structure of many of his compositions lends itself readily to adaptation to the guitar without loss of the original.

1. *Particular attention should be given to the right hand fingering given in the following measures. A repeat of the same finger would spoil the clarity of the passage.*

2. *Care should be taken to sustain the bass notes from this point through to the double bar. There is a natural tendency to lift the fingers holding the bass notes, but the passage is only effective if both parts are clear and sustained.*

3. *The ligado is made by hammering the G with the left hand fourth finger without playing it with the right hand. A less than ideal technique it is nevertheless audible in this position, and preferable to the alternative.*

Suggested tempo is ♩ = 184.

Domenico Scarlatti
(1685–1757)

62

Prelude

Although this piece is frequently played on keyboard instruments it was in fact originally written for the lute, the J. P. Kellner manuscript bearing the title *Praelude in C
moll pour la Lute di J. S. Bach.* It is an attractive arpeggio study which has long been a
favorite with guitarists.

1. *This half bar with the fourth finger is an unusual technique, but the only solution in
this case. It is important to note that the bass F only lasts for the first beat and does not
have to be sustained further. This means that the weight of the hand may be transfered
to the little finger when the first finger is raised from the F. Some players find the
passage easier to play with the first finger also in bar position.*

2. *The half bar should cover three strings only in preparation for the open D in the final
beat of the measure.*

3. *The half bar must here cover five strings.*

4. *An F in the bass of the original is assumed to be a copying error. The bar here should
cover four strings so that the first finger may slide smoothly to the fourth string A. It is
possible to play the whole measure with a bar, but this involves a very awkward stretch.*

5. *The same situation as note 4. A four string bar enables the first finger to slide to the F♯.*

6. *Note the change to an A bass here, often mistakenly delayed until the following measure.*

The tempo of a prelude is very much up to the player, and as a suggestion only I would
give ♩ = 92.

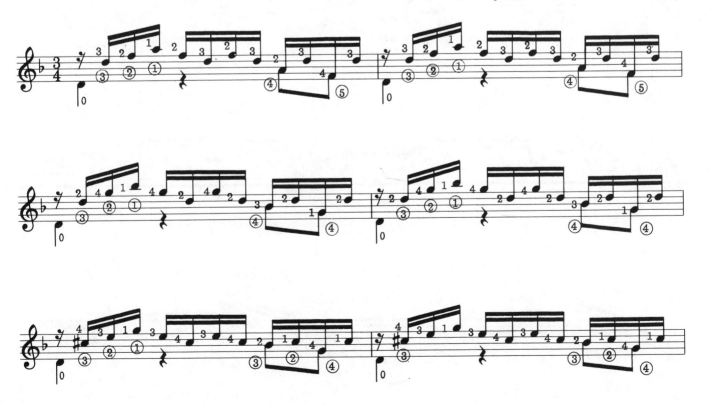

Johann Sebastian Bach

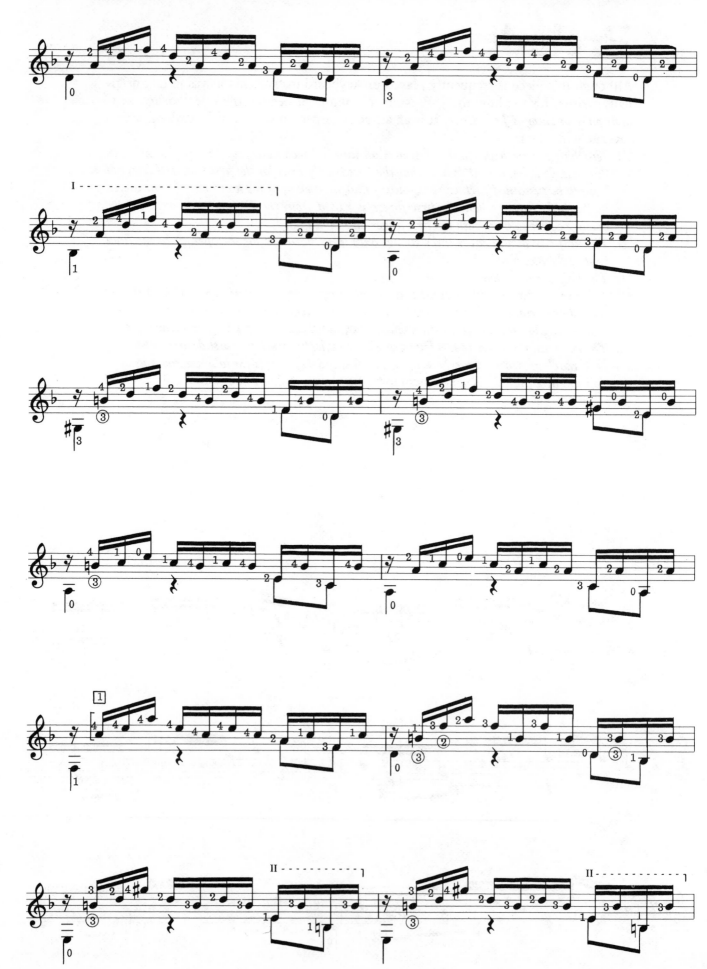

The Sense of Hearing, by Gregorius Fentzel, mid 17th century, Germany. The etching shows a lute, lyre, harp, bass viol, flutes, curved cornett, and cittern.

Sarabande

The following two pieces are from the Sonata in B minor (BWV1002) for unaccompanied violin. Although there is no known lute version of the Sonata the custom of the time of transferring music from one instrument to another makes it at least possible that it was played by the lutenists. For example the Suite in C minor for unaccompanied Violoncello, (BWV1011), exists also in a version for the lute in Bach's handwriting, with the title *Pieces pour la Luth a Monsieur Schouster par J. S. Bach.*

The sarabande sounds very natural on the guitar, and should be played with a broad sustaining quality.

1. *The slightly awkward fingering is necessary to sustain the bass C♯.*
2. *Place a full bar at this point in preparation for the low F♯.*

Suggested tempo is ♩ = 63.

Johann Sebastian Bach

Baroque music printing. Title page of *Clavier Sonaten Mit obligater Violine* by Johann Sebastian Bach

Double

The double should be paired with the preceding sarabande since it provides a variation to it built on the same harmonic structure. It is a masterly example of the broken style, whereby a series of single notes combine in the ear of the listener to form an impression of both melody and harmony. To enhance this effect the player may sustain arpeggiated notes which form a chord when the position of the hand permits. To give an example, in spite of the simple form of the writing the first measure might well be played:—

1   *Note that the D is taken on the third string, an interim move on the way up to the ninth position half bar.*

The tempo should be fast in contrast to the sarabande, about ♩. = 96.

Johann Sebastian Bach

Gavotte En Rondeau

This gavotte is from the suite in G minor (BWV995) here transposed to A minor. As mentioned in the note on p. 70, an autograph manuscript (now in the Bibliothèque Royale, Brussels) bears the title *Pieces pour la Luth a Monsieur Schouster, par J. S. Bach.*

1. *The half bar should be of three strings only so that the G# may be sustained.*
2. *The third finger must remain firmly in position on the G to facilitate the following slur.*
3. *A bass A in the original is impossible to sustain on the guitar. For this reason the initial A may be held over the first two beats of the measure to give a more positive sound to the cadence.*

Suggested tempo is ♩ = 100.

Johann Sebastian Bach

Art Thou Troubled?
(Dove Sei)

From the opera *"Rodelinda"*

Rodelinda was first performed on the 13th February 1725, and an account of the first night is given by W. S. Rockstro in his book *The Life of George Frederick Handel*, (London, Macmillan 1883).

> "Cuzzoni created so extraordinary a furore in this charming opera, that the brown silk gown, trimmed with silver, in which she performed the part of Leroine, led the fashion of the season. Senesino also won great and well-deserved applause by his interpretation of the accompanied recitative, *Pompe vani de morte,* and the following air *Dove Sei."*

The air has remained popular with vocalists, and is given here with an English lyric more expressive than a literal translation of the Italian.

Words by W. G. Rothery *

George Friedrich Handel
(1685–1759)

Largo

Art___ thou trou - bled? Mu - sic will calm thee, Art thou

---

* Reprinted by kind permission of Novello and Company, London.

wea - ry? Rest shall be thine, rest shall be thine.

Mu - sic, mu - sic source of all glad - ness,

heals thy sad - ness at her shrine, Mu - sic,

mu - sic, ev - er di - vine, Mu - sic,

mu - sic __ call -eth   with   voice __ di - vine.

This shows the First Lute part of the duo by Lauffensteiner transcribed on the following pages. *Staatsbibliothek, Augsburg, West Germany.*

Grave

Austrian-born Wolff Jacob Lauffensteiner was a lutenist in the household of Prince Ferdinand of Bavaria. His duties included such unrelated tasks as the purchase of his employer's wardrobe, and for instructing the Prince in music it is recorded that his salary was increased by 100 florins. Unfortunately as witnessed in a later petition by Lauffensteiner, this sum was mistakenly deducted from, rather than added to, his rather humble wage.

He appears not to have shared the freedom of travel enjoyed by other court lutenists of his time, having been obliged to accompany his employer even into battle; but with the Prince he had the opportunity to visit France and Italy.

Lauffensteiner composed for the solo lute, lute duet and also for small ensemble.

This duet and the two movements which follow are taken from a manuscript in the Staatsbibliothek, Augsburg (Tonk. Fasc. III, 5) entitled *Sonata a Liuto Primo et Secundo ou Violino, Viol de Gamba et Violoncello*. They make extremely effective guitar duets, and are not difficult to play.

[1] *In the original an identical bass is given to both lute parts probably for convenience when another single voiced instrument substituted for either part. For the purpose of allowing more melodic freedom to the upper part I have at times eliminated the double bass.*

[2] *In the original the B and F♯ were not dotted. However this kind of detail was often left to the understanding of the performer.*

[3] *The original has a half note A instead of the final two quarter notes.*

[4] *Here too the dotted notes are editorial, to match the pattern at the conclusion of the second half.*

[5] *Whichever form of trill is chosen both players should take care to play the same one, and to align the note values in each part. For this reason I would suggest a simple form of trill, such as:—*

[6] *The original half-note D has been changed to two quarter notes as in note [3]*
The small notes indicate appoggiaturas, which were used with such frequency that a number of them have been left unrealized so that the player may decide whether or not to include them. For information on this ornament see pp. 13 and 14 of the introduction.

As the title implies the tempo should be slow, ♩ = 76.

Grave

Wolff Jacob Lauffensteiner
(1676–1754)

Allegro

1 *I have made some minor rhythmic corrections to balance this statement to that of the upper part. The differences were quite possibly copying errors.*

2 *The bass has been transposed from the first to the second part for technical convenience.*

Suggested tempo is ♩ = 84.

Wolff Jacob Lauffensteiner

Andante

This very attractive andante translates readily to the guitar and should present few technical difficulties. As in the other movements I have at times left the bass in one part only where the doubling in unison did not seem to add any musical value.
Suggested tempo is a relaxed ♪ = 104.

Wolff Jacob Lauffensteiner

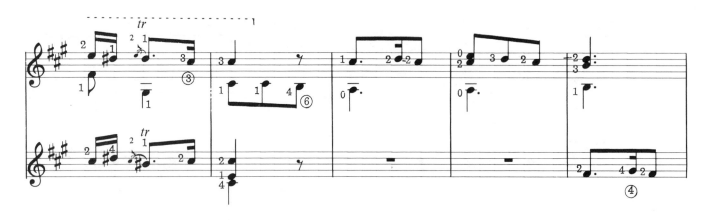

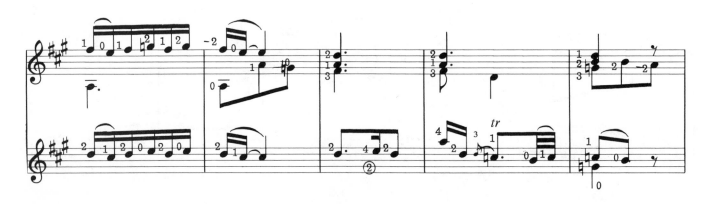

Passacaglia

The baroque passacaglia consisted of a series of variations around a subject usually introduced in the bass part. In this example the theme appears in the bass for the first half of the initial section and is concluded in the upper part. The following section does exactly the reverse.

The tempo should be moderately slow ♩ = 60, and the interpretation grand and dramatic but with contrasts. Arpeggiation should continue in the style of the first line.

1 *A simple realization of this trill would be:—*

However the slow tempo suggests a greater number of repetitions of the B♭ and A, the exact number being up to the discretion of the player. As a personal choice I would tend to stress the initial dissonance, thus:—

2 *Chords paired in this way would be played in the period with a thumb stroke for the first (accented) chord producing an arpeggiation from bass to treble. The weaker chord which follows would be played with an arpeggiation in the other direction (treble to bass) with one or more fingers.*

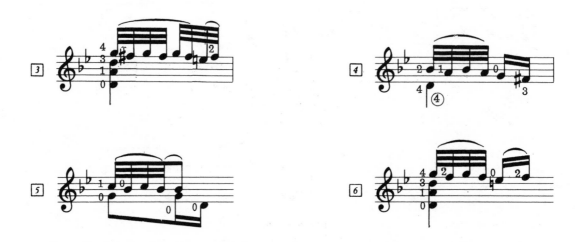

7 *The seemingly excessive trills which occur on the final beat of each measure from this point to the end of the piece have been omitted. Advanced players may wish to restore them but will have to adjust the fingering accordingly.*

Passacaglia

Lodovico Roncalli

Tombeau De M. Mouton (Allemande)

The word *Tombeau* was used to describe a piece written as a lament on the death of the dedicatee. This particular work (which I consider one of de Visée's finest) paid tribute to Charles Mouton, one of the most celebrated lutenists of his day who was also famous as a teacher. The original was for the lute, published in de Visée's last book *Pieces de Theorbe et de Luth*, Paris 1716, and a tablature version exists in the de Saizenay manuscript (Besançon Municipal Library).

The allemande was a very popular form with the French lutenists and guitarists. In ⁴⁄₄ time it was played at a stately tempo and conventionally commenced with a short upbeat. By this period it had ceased to be danced, and as a stylized movement of the suite followed the initial prelude.

I would suggest a slow brooding approach to bring out the melancholy quality of the piece ♩ = 66.

2 *The fingering may seem complex here, but once understood the passage is very simple to play.*

3 *An awkward change to the next chord, but notice that the second finger remains on the E.*

4 *This hollow—sounding chord might appear to be a mistake (due to the absence of a third), but it appears in both the published and manuscript versions.*

Robert de Visée

Allemande

Amongst the famous player-composers of the Baroque guitar Corbetta is listed by Gaspar Sanz in his book of 1674 *Instrucción de musica sobre la guitarra Espanola* as "the best of all." He was a court musician to Louis XIV and also to Charles II where he taught the instrument to many of the nobility. So popular did the guitar become that the English court scene was described as one of "universal strumming."

Corbetta's music is designed very specifically for the five-course double-stringed baroque guitar, and a full realization is only possible on this instrument. The Allemande below is at best a transcription, but will serve to give some idea of the curious style and originality of this celebrated musician. It was first printed in a major collection of Corbetta's entitled *La Guitare Royale*, Paris 1671.

1. *The arrows show the characteristic direction of arpeggiation of these repeated chords.*
2. *Corbetta's music is liberally spiced with trills, which can become monotonous to the modern ear. Some may perhaps be simplified to appoggiaturas, but it would be a mistake to omit the introductory note altogether. Alternatives to a long trill here would be:—*

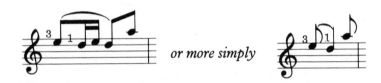

3. *Trills on quarter-notes are noted simply* ⌇ *to distinguish them from more important cadential trills. However they would still commence with the note above, and are probably best rendered thus:—*

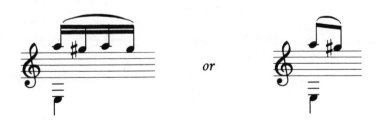

4. *The trill on the inner string was quite common in Corbetta's music.*
5. *Although quite a stretch is involved the unusual trill is effective.*

The suggested tempo is ♩ = 88.

Allemande

Francesco Corbetta
(1620–1681)

Sarabande And Variations

Unfortunately Handel is not known to have written for the solo lute, though the theorbo would have been frequently used for the continuo accompaniment of his songs. He specified the lute and theorbo for the accompaniment of one of the arias in the *Ode to St. Cecilia* and in several other major works.

The sarabande below is a keyboard piece, but is a favorite among guitarists because of the skillful working of the theme *La Folia*, one of the most popular folk melodies in Western music. The origin of *La Folia* is lost in obscurity, though its similarity with *La Romanesca* makes it certainly Spanish, as is borne out by its other title *Folias de España*.

The guitar version is quite demanding on the left hand and definitely not for beginners.

1. *It may be found helpful to take the G with the first finger in bar position in preparation for the chord.*
2. *Note that a full bar is necessary at this point.*
3. *The bar at the fifth fret should be a full one in preparation for the move to the full bar at the eighth fret.*
4. *A five string bar is probably the best here, as a full bar would make it almost impossible to reach the F with the fourth finger. In fact the reach is considerably easier when the piece is played up to time as the note passes quickly.*
5. *The third finger reach is difficult, but also passes more easily when the piece is played up to time.*

Suggested tempo for the theme is a grandiose ♩ = 58.

6th to D

George Friedrich Handel

Variation I

Variation II

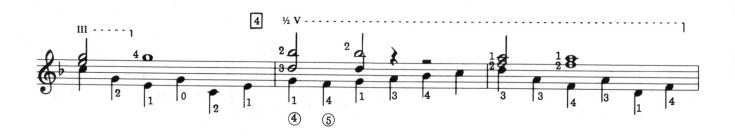

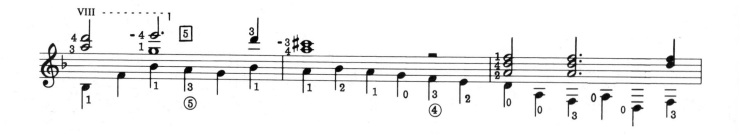

Fair Celia

John Blow was one of the leading composers of the Restoration, who as a choirboy of the Chapel Royal was already composing anthems that were considered good enough to be performed by the choir. He was somewhat overshadowed by his illustrious pupil Henry Purcell, whom he succeeded as organist of Westminster upon the latter's death in 1695, but nevertheless attained considerable celebrity, particularly with his sacred music.

In 1700 he published a collection of secular songs entitled *Amphion Anglicus,*(Playford, 1700),probably motivated by the success of the *Orpheus Brittanicus,* a similar collection of Purcell's songs published two years earlier. This song is a particularly attractive example from that collection.

The guitar accompaniment is derived from the bass which was figured for the *Organ, Harpsichord or Theorboe—Lute.*

Dr. John Blow
(1648–1708)

101

pas - sion_ feign. Tell me no more,_ no more_ you love;

can they pre - tend_ to love, who do re - fute what love_ per -

suades _ them to? Tell me no more,_ no more_ you

love who once_ has_ felt_ his ac - tive_ fire,_ dull

laws of honour will disdain; tell me no more, no more you love in vain, fair Celia, you would be thought, you would be thought, you would be thought his slave; and yet you will not, and yet you will not to his power submit.

Tell me no more,— no more— you love; in vain,— fair Ce - lia,

in vain— fair Ce - lia, you — this pas - sion feign.

Theorbe
This illustration from a manual of early instruments shows the Theorbo lute with its extended neck to give resonance and depth to the bass strings. *Weiderfeld & Nicolson.*

Sonata

Sylvius Leopold Weiss
(1686-1750)

Weiss was the most important lute composer of the late Baroque school, and the large number of his works surviving in manuscript are a fertile source for guitarists.

As a young man he visited Rome in the entourage of the Polish Prince Alexander Sobiesky, and later appointments in Dusseldorf, Dresden, Munich and Vienna, brought him into contact with some of the most famous musicians of the time including Joachim Quantz, Johann Fux (whose opera company he joined for a period as Theorbo-player) and J. S. Bach.

In 1722 an ugly scene with a violinist resulted in the latter biting his thumb so severely that he was unable to play for some months. He died in Dresden in 1750 leaving a wife and seven children.

There has been confusion for some years about the character of Weiss' music due to the attribution to him of a suite in the baroque style composed by the late Manuel Ponce. However the recent attention given to his genuine works by many performers has helped to correct the false impression.

The sonata below is from the manuscript collection in the Sächsische Landesbibliothek, Dresden. (Mus MS. 2841, V. 1.)

The two minuets are elementary in technique, and for this reason do not have separate study notes.

One of a set of Prints of the 5 Senses: **Hearing** A. Basse
Baroque music-making; a well-to-do family sings to the typical accompaniment of lute and viola da gamba. *The Trustees of the British Museum.*

Prelude

The prelude to a lute suite was a free form which served the dual purpose of an introduction and a check of the instruments tuning. Frequently the barring was omitted, as in the original of this prelude, giving a further impression of an improvisational piece.

[1] *The second finger on the D is awkward, but necessary to release the third finger for the following B. The stretch between F♯ and G which follows is difficult but possible with practice.*

[2] *Note the third finger on the A where you would expect to use the second. It is important that the second finger be free for the bass B which follows.*

[3] *The somewhat unusual fingering in this measure is not hard to play once it is clearly understood. It should be repeated until a clear mental picture is formed.*

[4] *The series of chords may be freely arpeggiated.*

Suggested tempo is ♩ = 76.

106

Allemande

For this allemande I would suggest a moderate tempo, ♩ = 100. It is one of the best pieces in the sonata, and also presents the most technical challenge, particularly in the second half.

[1] *To avoid a difficult change to the seventh position bar the first finger should take the B in bar position, but with the tip of the finger raised to allow the open D to sound.*

[3] *The indication here is of a natural harmonic, formed by touching the third string at the 12th fret. The harmonic will sustain as the hand moves to prepare the D with the third finger.*

[4] *A bar of five strings seems the least awkward here in preparation for the change to the second and fourth fingers in the following measure. This progression contains the major difficulty of the piece.*

[5] *The change to a full bar from a half bar is important in preparation for the move to the seventh position.*

[6] *At this point lift the end of the bar to allow the open strings to sound without releasing the B. A five string bar is the best for this purpose.*

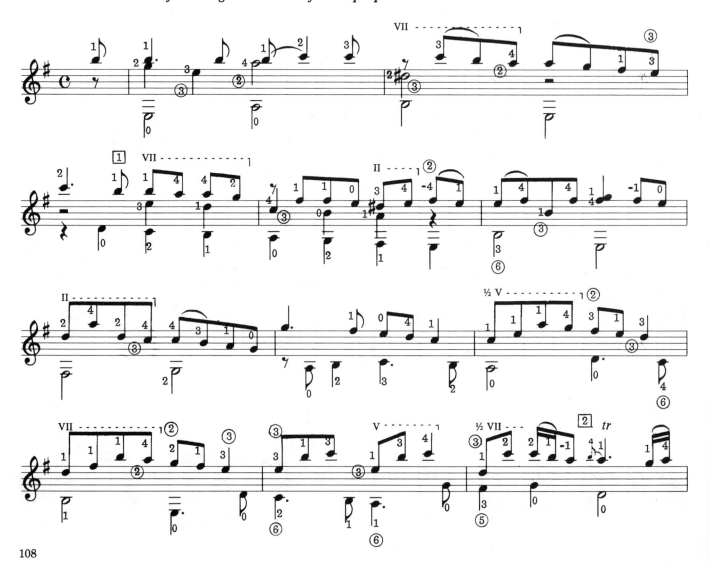

Courante

I would suggest a fast, flowing interpretation of the courante to make a distinct contrast with the allemande and bourrée, with a tempo about ♩ = 126 .

1⃞ *The second finger should remain on the E until the end of the following measure. This takes much of the difficulty out of this rather tricky opening.*

2⃞ *The third finger on the B may seem awkward, but is placed in preparation for the trill. For the latter I suggest:—*

3⃞ *The third finger should remain on the D♯ in preparation for the slur which follows.*

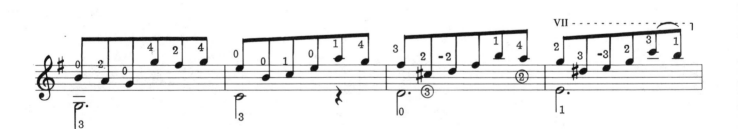

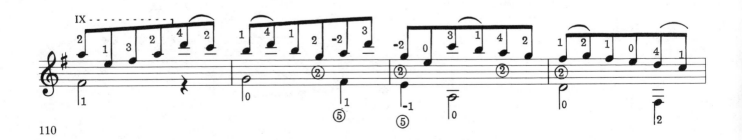

Sarabande

Suggested tempo is a stately $\quad \downarrow = 72 \quad$ for this piece, which is extremely effective if played with full tone quality and regard for sustained notes.

The first finger plays the D# and slides up to sound the E.

Bourrée

Suggested tempo for the Bourrée is allegro moderato, ♩ = 168.

[1] *The following two measures are not difficult to play, but the positions involved are somewhat hard to memorize. I would suggest special attention to the section and care in observing the correct fingering.*

[2] *A firm stroke is necessary for the whole note to sustain. The middle voice may be played more lightly in order to separate it from the melody.*

[3] *The high B with the first finger is awkward after the full bar. A useful solution for this situation is to use the side of the finger, raising only the end of the bar so as to sound the open A. The B is in fact played with the same part of the first finger as it would be in a full bar situation.*

Facsimile of baroque lute tablature

This Menuet (Minuet) by S. L. Weiss is transcribed on page 115. *Sächsische Landesbibliothek, Dresden, German Democratic Republic.*

Minuet I

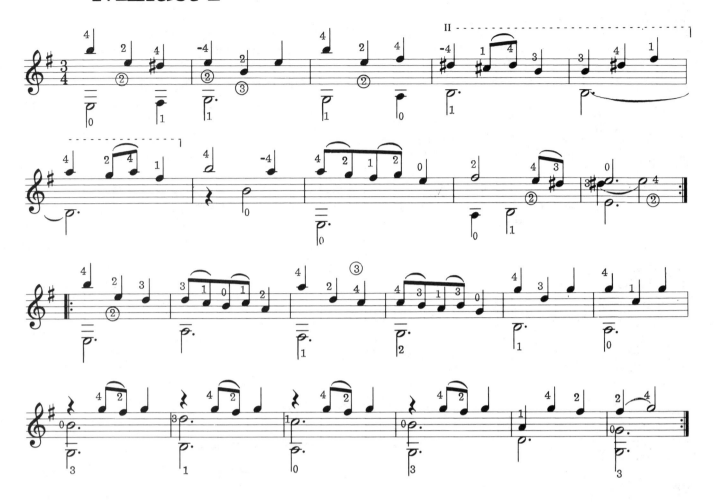

Minuet II

Gigue

To conclude the sonata with a flourish I would suggest a very lively tempo ♩. = 108 and a strong rhythmic approach. When the same passage appears twice, as in the second and third measures, the second time may be effectively taken as an echo.

1. *The F♯ is best taken with the side of the first finger as if it were barring, to avoid an awkward leap across the B. In effect the third position bar is moved down one fret, and the tip of the finger raised to allow the open A to sound.*

2. *The effect of an extra voice may be given by considering the initial bass note of this measure and the three which follow it as dotted half notes, so that the notes sustain throughout each measure.*

3. *To negotiate the difficult change from the fourth to the seventh position it is most important that the fourth finger be left on the second string and used to guide the hand as it moves from the F♯ to G.*

Passacaille

This passacaille takes the form of a series of variations on a fixed bass or ground. The aria-like first theme is repeated with minor variations at the conclusion.

As the one unifying thread throughout the piece is the bass line it is particularly important to keep this consistent with regard to sustained notes and balance. The fingering takes this into account, and is for this reason sometimes slightly unconventional in deference to a musical effect.

1. *Note that the fourth finger does not remain on the A, which would make the following E and A impossible while sustaining the bass C#.*

2. *The first finger reaches around the second for the high B, awkward, but the only solution if the bass B is to sustain.*

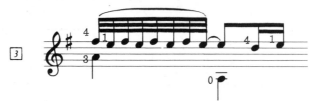

The suggestion above is not intended to be completely literal as far as the number of notes in the trill, but to show its completion a fraction before the low A. I would suggest a stress on the first F#.

4. *In this variation the first of each group of sixteenth notes may be taken as an additional (middle) voice, and accordingly emphasized and sustained where possible throughout the group.*

5. *The unusual fingering of the A and F# is to make the double ligado possible. The third and fourth fingers both pull off to sound the note prepared by the first and second fingers. This unusual technique is effective and not particularly difficult.*

6. *This measure affords an example of the style known as* Campanelas *(Bells) because of the overring from one string to another. It was idiomatic to both the guitar and lute of the Baroque period.*

7. *It is unfortunately not possible to sustain the bass through the first two beats of the measure while at the same time allowing the E which begins the second beat to ring through the arpeggio. As the notes marked with an accent seem to imply an extra voice here I have fingered the passage to allow them to sustain.*

Suggested tempo for the theme is ♩ = 66.

Sylvius Leopold Weiss

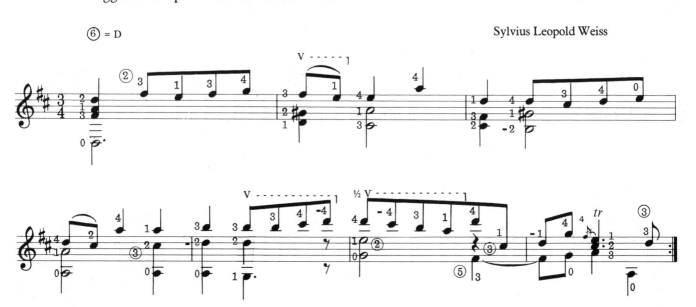

119

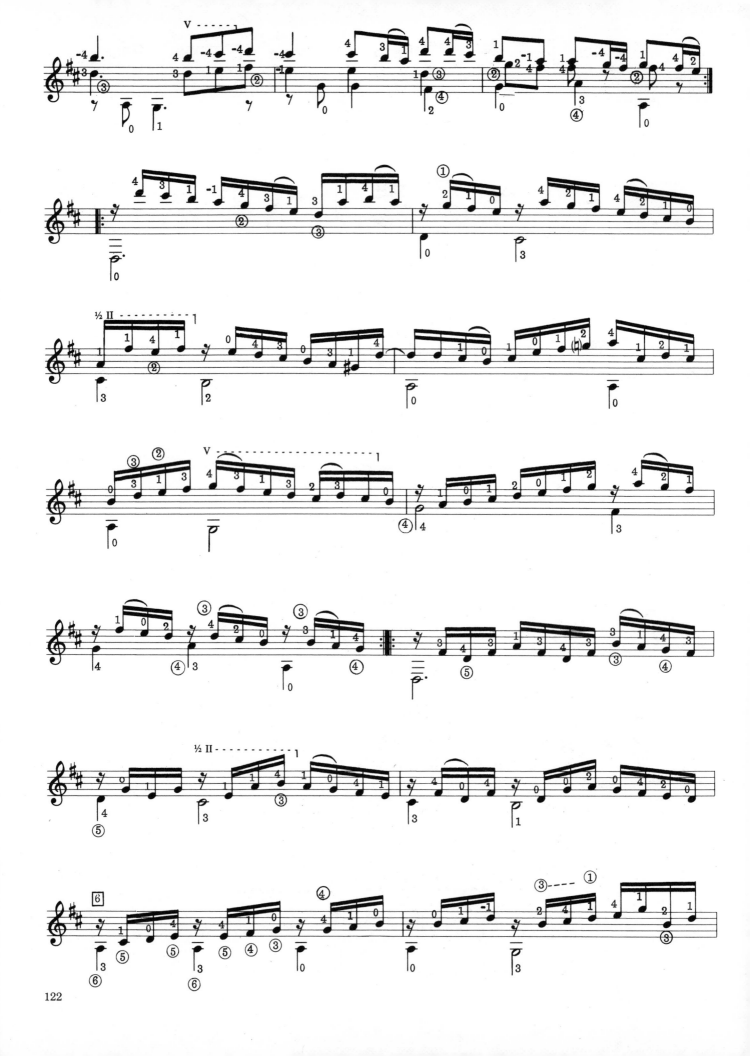

122

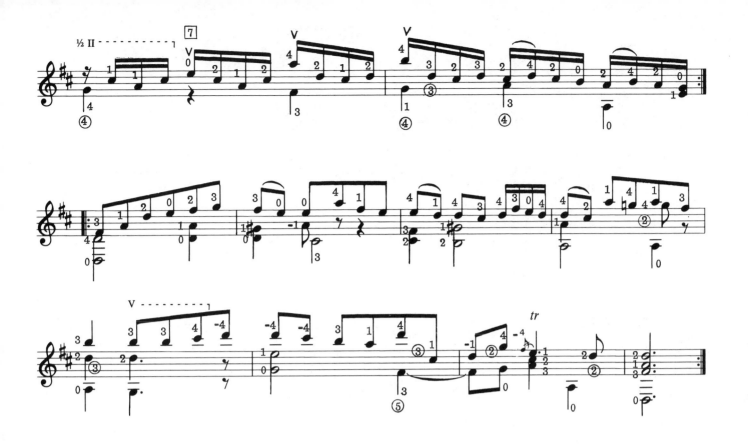

Facsimile of baroque lute tablature
From the manuscript of S. L. Weiss. This piece is transcribed on page 118. *The Trustees of the British Museum.*

Tombeau Sur La Mort De M. Comte De Logy

This memorial to Count Losy von Losinthal is one of Weiss' finest pieces. It has a tragic majesty that is extremely expressive, and in spite of its comparative complexity translates well to the guitar.

1. *The difficult change to this chord is facilitated if the fourth finger remains firmly on the E as the other fingers find their place around it.*
2. *The ornament intended here is not clear, but may be taken as a mordent, e.g.*

In this case the following mordents would be from B to A♯, A♯ to G♯ and B to A♯. Although I have no supporting evidence I am not entirely convinced that Weiss did not intend simply a stressed vibrato on these notes.

3. *The fourth finger move from the high A to the G on the fourth string is less than ideal fingering, but there is no logical alternative.*
4. *The first mordent is written out as the pattern for the following ones indicated by the sign (⨈).*
5. *Place the bar on the G♯ at this point, but with the end of the finger clear of the open D. It may then be dropped into the full bar position for the following chord.*
6. *An effective realization of this difficult ornament is given in a fine recording by Julian Bream* Julian Bream/Baroque Guitar, RCA Victor LSC-2878 *as follows.*

Although the marked ornaments stop at the first group of the next measure he logically continues this pattern throughout the two measures until the texture of the music changes.

7. *Note that the second position bar is placed for the final C♯ of the measure, and that this does not damp the bass notes.*

The suggested tempo is ♪ = 56.

Tombeau Sur La Mort De
M. Comte De Logy

Sylvius Leopold Weiss